ABRAXAS

# PEPE BELMONTE
## POEMS/PROSE/PICTURES

HERMIT'S BOOKS
Somewhere by The Sea

## AKNOWLEDGEMENTS

Thanks are due to David Swetenham, Jenny Lindfors, Beth Humphries, Ian M Hale, Fareed Sahloul, Lorna Rose, Grace Banks, Dear Pariah, Adeel Aktar, Guen Murroni and The Three Magdalenas.

An audio recording of the complete reading with musical accompaniment *ought* to accompany this book. Plans for it's availability as a digital download from the usual places including Pepe's website are in motion.

These are a collection of works conceived before March 2011.

"These Christ's that die upon the barricade
God knows it I am with them in some things."

O. W.

Thanks so much
Andrew

Ed

Pepe

# CONTENTS

I owe Charlie

## I Must Create

It seems I am in love with you again.
It just happened and evolved this time
As a deep sisterly kinship.

There is a picture of her as a child
In the Basque country I think.
The fingers of one hand are in her mouth,
Head lowered slightly,
Eyes protective and hooded.
A defensive poise;
A child unsure
Of alien market folk.

Regardless Rose, quick to think and quick to trot.
I endeavour to let the songbird be
And, in hand should she stay,

I would rejoice and be contented.

Alas, I must still create

Here lies the carcass of a man undone.

See how the body lies;
Arms crossed over his heart
And the teeth clenched tight.
The last moment caught before his soul died.

Yet see there, between the teeth,
A flower red and true,
Still fresh as the day 'twas picked,
Failing to succumb, stubborn even.
And there entwined between fingers
A chain of delicate gold and amber;
A locket for the love undone.

The jackals have fled,
The vultures have long gone,
Here lies the carcass of a man undone.

I should have fought that man today but not like the time when the Jeep driver pulled a U-turn in front of the motorbike. That was all shock, emotion and fear. A few puffs on a cigarette sorted that one out. This one was different. This one wanted fists and loose teeth but I didn't know why. He was deliberate and he called me a coward for walking away.

After he said it her words and her hips started to blur and lose their meaning. They ceased to appease me and I still wish I'd smacked him round the head so I could at least forget about it even though I might have lost some teeth.

Women call courage what men call cowardice;
A mystery I love but don't understand.

A wild horse that's been trying to throw me off
Is suddenly calm.
I caught her months ago
Yet only tonight was she made tame,
Only tonight did she take my whip and bit,
Only tonight could I call her my mine,
And before this night we were at war.

I can continue now and
I am relieved.
Pass my thanks to those who kept watch,
The reigns are taught,
She's ready and we must make our leave.

Betrayal

There's this thorn in my paw, see.
It's been making me limp.
I got a text message from David saying,
"I'm going to the cinema with Goliath tonight.
Don't wait up."
Can you believe it?

It feels like God sniggering,
Holding the pins
Of all the grenades I'm juggling.

An accordion in the courtyard plays.
The film people gave him a new identity and cut his hair
and now his head feels like it's wearing him rather than the
other way around. I have to shave everyday too.
So, with his new 'hip' head, cultural squalls defy him and he
is forced to recalibrate for the sake of being able to afford
the rent; measuring and serving himself up again and again
and again...

## Cigarette

It starts with a sibilant sin,
Falters for a second by the obstinate gate
But soon settles after ignition;
And whips us away on a snarling V8,
Two-tone, black top, straight white line combustion dream,
Promises nothing and pulls it all
Toward any smouldering accomplishment you want.

Your head is always in your hands.
Your lap is always warm with another's weight.
Your deaths are never fulfilled.
And your glass is half empty each time it's refilled.

Dear Mother Island,

Whose inspiration did cascade
From ancient wells of potent knowledge,
I have to leave your side.

Left alone I am un-consoled,
And I search not in that
Direction you would have wished.
Any, but the path I tread
You have guided me toward.
Alas, here I stand with my soiled heart spread.
I've done that which a son should but dream of doing;
Cast stones against your wild stained glass,
Expecting satisfaction from each broken coloured shard,
Only to be heart-broken, rendered speechless,
When, after questioning gaze,
You stooped and began again to rebuild, honouring Kipling!
And so much more we learnt,
And there was numerous cost.
I'll never be the innocence you so rightly deserved
And to me, since that smashing day
I'll see you in another light.

No forgiveness can comprehend
That which was first thrown.

I love thee Mother Island.

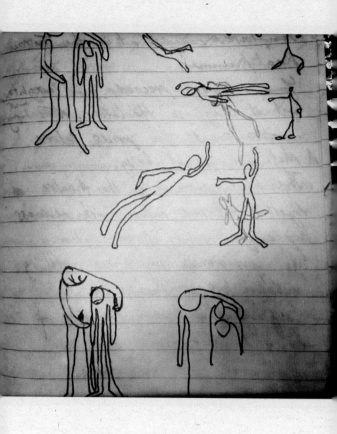

One day, perhaps in autumn we'll meet again. By a train station, or a fast food take away, or a cinema queue, a gig, the supermarket and somewhere else; we'll know when we're there. I believe we've already met. Your medieval aura preceded you and it was as though I sensed the past approaching, my history walking toward me through the amber light behind Kings Cross.

You spoke.
"You look incredibly familiar."

Your name, your body, your hair, your face was backlit. I couldn't see you. I was smoking outside with a delicate thought (that I was no longer young), which was whispered away with your words, allowing discreet and silent rooms of my soul great illumination. Your command met my necessity. I couldn't see you and, like I said, we knew. But I didn't know where to go. Paralysed and unprepared. And soon, and too soon as swiftly as enlightenment is revealed it is daubed and doubted and I was again within myself without you.

I sat much the same then as I do today. Perhaps I'll remain this way, stoic and unchanged, like our unfurled flag; just in case. Perhaps I'll climb as high as I can, whenever I can and be a swooping flag or an atom or something similar. Her changes will happen unconscious of mine. I'll change; I'll evolve as an ever-loving chameleon fearsome, lonely and kind.

We were unconsciously comparing and challenging each other's worlds; over excited and beautifully cursed in our fleshy shells of self-conviction and humour tinged with hostility. I thanked her for being there, perhaps that was the mistake because when my premonition was confirmed what a noise she made about it. I tried to keep it between us but she couldn't help sharing and it slipped away. It became diluted and I didn't recognise her when she came around again with the vampire twins. It must have been a the half-hearted engagement from the start.

Their love is a flame upon a candle,
In a room without a breeze.
Poised and stoic white and still.
Its seems obvious to me,
Like de Beauvoir's poppy
Or Zarathustra's thrill
That it is bound
To extinguish itself.

March 6th 2006 12.18pm

On a boring train from Waterloo, south bound and drunk.
I forget their stop, who cares which stop it was years ago...

The lights go down. The curtain sways slightly. The
spotlights focus. There they are. They appear; revealed in
all their roaring simplicity. Right down to the bare bones.
How we loved it. Dumb passengers about to be given a
piece of working theatre Artaud and Boal would have been
proud of. The couple are drunk and giggly together.

With a slovenly grace she has stumbled to the carriage
floor. Catching herself on one knee she gazes up at him and
with this simple gesture she has proposed.

Now we're all waiting. Tender-hooks. Everyone together on
that aimless boring carriage, waiting. Why are we always
waiting? Even when it's happening we're waiting.

The train keels gently from side to side. An imperceptible
motion swaying us all in a nodding unison, clicking its iron
fingers and wooden thumbs in time. Jazz. The garish
fluorescent light dragging romance to one side like a
naughty schoolboy but its too late and we all want a show.
We all want a drama. We've invested our own love now,
don't you see?

"Time passes quick," she says, brazenly, honestly. "What
else is there, Hun? C'mon."
  "Yeah, go on!" I think. But what do I know?

Violence is suddenly on the cards. He's angry because he
feels she's putting him on the spot in public. But it's not like
that to her. *He* is everything. It's, "their tedium up against

28

our beauty, babe" and "battling with curses over spilt milk" as far as she's concerned. As long as I've got my man.

"Nothing but promises of new beginnings," she retorts steadily, lovingly. "They lost everything when they gave us the libraries." I'm nodding. I think she must be crazy. I think she must be wonderful.

I'm just about to stand up and shout, "I do" when I am asked for my ticket. The last train outta Nowhere Town and I'm still negotiating with dull authority. Torn from my reverie and fumbling through pockets I suddenly remember how I felt meeting your friend last week and I say out loud,

"You could be a terrorist with friends like that."

If she could see me now writing and smoking at three in the
morning fearful of our face and volume

...she told me over an awful piece of meat (we both enjoyed with glee and relish) about her childhood. A letter she sent to her aunt about the fraught relationship between her mother and father and that this letter was the reason her father divorced her mother. And about how when a high profile priest was assassinated in the early Polish 80s, his body thrown in the boot of a government car and dumped in the river. How, at age 5 she would be terrified that his murderers were hiding in the wardrobe along the corridor leading to her bedroom and she would have to run past it to get to bed for fear of getting caught. She had a dream about me also but told me she couldn't tell me what it was about; only that it was a good dream. We spoke about unconditional love, about being free from social constraints and it scared me. I withdrew. She was talking politics and it upset me. I couldn't follow and lost myself thinking of stupid idioms. She warned me to be careful, "I'm a fire snake", she said. But perhaps me being a water sign is enough, I thought. I may extinguish something in her. She certainly danced like a fire-snake. She asked me how long I wanted to live for. I told her it was the wrong question, and felt upset again. She'd been knowingly with the wrong man for 8 years; telling him she may meet someone else; he saying it was okay; and she'd suggested already that they get married. And finally, she did meet someone else. Now she's as independent as they come. Lives alone in a cupboard in H. P. with mushrooms growing from the damp and the cold. A-life-model-and-a-model-of-life. She was reading a J. D. biography, brimming full of yearning, desperation for understanding. It rang so vivid it made me want to try my hand at desperation and for that I can truly thank her...

11th.nov.2008

34

Trains pass by
In gentle melancholy
I still owe people money

It's a thin moral fixture
That taints the gate of trust
And saddens friendships
Which can't wait

Finishing my lodger's chocolate
I'm distracted yet enthused
I didn't doubt that we understood each other
Though they'll try to scheme it like we did

For the fate of friendship to be resting on
Such a small sum owed is ludicrous
And maddening to me
Yet I don't fail to see their angles

And I hate it when my reputation
Precedes me

Lost

The world is an island
Flooded with boundaries,
Like the London of my dreams,
Never really existing anywhere.
Another damsel in distress.
I pass on what I can.
I live my life that way.
The choices already made for me.
And the mayflies have long gone
With September's cunning air.

While the death of springtime
Is happening outside
Two hearts lay beating
Wide awake and naked
With nowhere to hide
A pendant with its chimes
Of memories and rhymes
Lies crushed and thwarted
Its silver casing having turned blue
-

It's the coming of the autumn
There's nothing left in season
Not one fruit that sits well with me
Across from this table
A young man is acting able
But the mob can tell he's afraid
They're allured by the scent
And the way he's holding his cup
-

The coffee stains slowly get replaced
When the red wine starts to flow
And the priest starts to leave
Whispering his blessing in haste

If we could fly above the clouds
the sun would always shine.

We'd be caught in wave,
But left in a daze,
Of a world unmade,
Un-gathered and unordered
Like a life without borders:
Constantly crossed, constantly gored.

Consider privacy
And we become anxious.

Childlike kinship permeates communicado.
The ether of converse striving toward notions like
"We Must Be Happy."

'Lightness of being' prevails
With talk of 'bigger', 'lofty' and 'heavy' things
Abruptly being
Dismissed as notions of grandeur.

Ironically maybe, the claim made
In defence of your own
Lifestyle and life choices
Is one of liberal artistry.

How we would suffer should we agree!
And how we do unwittingly suffer
Since we oblige agreement,
Fearing each other's opinions.

I'll happily be served,
Its just I have such little faith in the service.

the trees are shedding their leaves
too soon if you ask me
and too soon for you too
I'm going to try to go to sleep

"It's a shame," she said looking back over her shoulder as I stood in the darkened room. The Black Narcissus of dreams regretfully realised and working woman of sorrow and heart. The memory is more than simply cold in my bed.

It wasn't my bed.

Surprise when I kiss your mouth, and surprise at that recoil was all we truly shared. Crossing boundaries I never cared to know and so I withdrew deep into the male in me.

Despite the gesture it was never a gift; more like blackmail.
The compromise has evolved perhaps as it should.
Less expensive some would say.

## Well-Heeled Amianto

The graveyard shift came to me late,
At an unholy hour
With it's ancient craft to honour.
I was lost at the time,
Trapped among boys in men's bodies,
Confined to a night of unguarded lust by a feeble pioneer.
What I was shown as camaraderie
I saw as something altogether frightening.
Horror after horror.

After the masks, the trench, the fast food,
The B.S. and the bull came the hospital.
I remember your twins in the prem unit.
They were dead three days later.
Back in the trenches I thought
Our own solemn breathing apparatus
Hopelessly incarnated theirs.
I remember driving the Transit past a funeral home too.
The miniature headstones in the window
Triggered your pain and your reckless compassion
At the possibilities for your dead offspring.

Your disordered heart mute and breaking
And me endeavouring to hold it
With something mirroring Love.

Dear darling,
I promise tomorrow
*I will* lay down the deposit.
*I will* consider my future.
I *will* consider drinking more.
(Of course, I meant to say *drinking less!*)
Tonight I've decided to do these things tomorrow, darling.

## A Song For Amy

No-one knows my name
Love is a losing game
I just can't help myself
I caught a Southern bird
Red lace caught my eye
White silk keeps me from crying
You're all out of sight
I'm never out of my mind

Before too long
Secrets become
Friend's conversation
My lonesome prince
Stares at the altar
As if it's something that he's never seen

They put me on trial
Before I knew my crime
Caught out and let down
You're on your own now
But I tread water well
And I have my father's hands
And I know my time
Will treat me kind

They're calling me
Little Misanthropy
Without any notion
Or care or devotion
Love is a losing game
Hate is such a darn shame
So I won't mind losing some
For this soul won't be tamed